Original title:
Sunlit Shores

Copyright © 2025 Creative Arts Management OÜ
All rights reserved.

Author: Eleanor Prescott
ISBN HARDBACK: 978-1-80581-494-8
ISBN PAPERBACK: 978-1-80581-021-6
ISBN EBOOK: 978-1-80581-494-8

Chasing the Horizon

On the beach, I run and trip,
Mimicking a seals' wild flip.
I chase the waves, they tease me near,
Splashing water from ear to ear.

A crab takes off, I try to follow,
But he's too fast—now this feels hollow.
Sandy shorts and a sunburned nose,
I laugh at how this madness grows.

Lighthouses in Laughing Light

The lighthouse stands, a cheerful chap,
Winking at ships, it's got the clap.
With its beam, it guides the lost,
But often it sneezes—what a cost!

Seagulls argue, no end in sight,
Poking fun at the goofy light.
"Oh look, there's a ship, it's headed straight!"
The lighthouse chuckles, "Well, isn't that great?"

Iridescent Surf

The waves chat lightly, it's all a game,
"Hey, bring me a seashell with your name!"
They crash and tumble, with witty remarks,
A frothy laugh, like playful sharks.

A beach ball rolls past, it looks quite giddy,
Bouncing around, oh isn't that silly?
Sandcastles frown, their walls a mess,
"Why take life seriously? It's just the press!"

Cobalt Skies and Warm Sands

Under cobalt skies, I lay with a grin,
Counting the seagulls as they spin.
One steals my sandwich, the cheeky lad,
I shout, "Hey, that's my lunch you cad!"

The sands tickle toes, making me squeal,
While sunscreen attacks, oh what a deal!
I slip on a flip-flop, take a wild leap,
And face-plant right—oh, dreams aren't cheap!

Morning's Gentle Caress

The rooster crows with all its might,
While seagulls plan their dawn delight.
Coffee spills in clumsy hands,
As dreams get lost in beachy sands.

A crab dances in a little jig,
With tiny legs, oh, what a gig!
The sun climbs high, the sunblock flies,
As people trip in silly guise.

Reflections of Hope

A surfer wipes out, but grins nonetheless,
His friends all laugh, it's quite the mess.
The waves roll in with awkward cheer,
While seagulls swoop, oh dear, oh dear!

Beach balls bounce, they soar and land,
Who knew fun could be so unplanned?
A toddler's tantrum, a splash of sand,
Makes for memories, hilariously grand.

An Opalescent Day

Sandy toes and laughter loud,
Umbrellas like mushrooms, they form a crowd.
A pinwheel spins on a warm breeze,
As sunscreen gets sticky with all of these!

Flip-flops fly in a crazy race,
As salted hair decorates each face.
A seagull steals a snack with flair,
And everyone shrieks, 'Hey, that's not fair!'

Ethereal Beachside Echoes

The tide rolls in with a playful tease,
Splashing everyone, big and small, with ease.
A dog digs deep for a lost treasure,
While kids build castles with carefree pleasure.

Sunscreen battles leave everyone white,
As laughter echoes into the night.
With goofy poses, selfies abound,
Memories made, oh, laughter's found!

Breezes That Hold the Sun

A seagull swoops, it steals my hat,
The wind just laughs, how about that?
Flip-flops fly with every gust,
Who knew sunbathing was such a must?

I drop my drink, it spills with flair,
Chasing ice cubes, I run with care.
The sand is hot, I hop and shout,
Next time, I'll pick a place without a drought!

The Dance of Light

The rays come down, a silly wiggle,
My shadow dances, what a jiggle!
Laughter echoes, crabs join the fun,
Who knew beach time could feel like a run?

Sunburned noses, red as a rose,
We slather on lotion, oh, how it glows!
Surfers tumble, they crash and splat,
With waves and giggles, imagine that!

Coral Shades and Summer Skies

Bright fish swim in colors bold,
Slipped on my goggles, I'm feeling sold!
The ocean whispers jokes in bubbles,
While shells play tricks, oh what troubles!

I try to float, but then I sink,
Bubbles burst forth like I'm on the brink.
With laughter loud, I splash around,
In this watery realm, true joy is found!

Timeless Vistas

The horizon stretches, oh what a view,
But where's my towel? I must pursue!
Kites tangled up, like a wild prank,
Even the sun seems to laugh, I think!

Sandcastles fall, they crumble down,
While I laugh hard, wearing a crown.
Golden hour comes, with shadows in tow,
Who knew chaos could steal the show!

The Call of the Sun-kissed Sea

A seagull stole my sandwich, oh dear,
While I was napping, no picnic cheer!
The waves just giggled, did they conspire?
To make my lunch float, oh, what a liar!

Sandcastle towers, I built with pride,
Only to see them washed away with the tide.
A crab waltzes by, looking quite grand,
I laugh while it pinches my ankle—unplanned!

Radiances of an Endless Summer

Flip-flops flopping, but one's missing a toe,
I hop around awkwardly, stealing the show.
Beach balls are bouncing, kids running amok,
One ended up stuck in a sunbather's sock!

Ice cream melting faster than I can devour,
Sticky fingers waving, oh what a dower!
A seagull swoops in for a sugar high,
While I scream, "Not today!" and watch it fly.

Shimmering Pathways

Sandy toes and giggles, a path so bright,
But oh, what's this? A jellyfish fright!
I dodge in confusion, a slip and a slide,
While laughter erupts like a joyful tide!

Buried treasure, or so I declare,
A lost flip-flop, a hazard, beware!
With every wave, the ocean takes back,
What it gave me last summer, oh, what a knack!

Tales of the Ocean's Glow

A clam told me secrets about the sea,
But all I could hear was its shell's decree.
I swore it grinned while the waves came to play,
Chasing my hat which had decided to sway!

Starfish a-scoffing at my awkward dance,
While dolphins giggle in a splashing prance.
"Join us!" they shout - I give it a go,
Only to trip and meet the ocean's flow!

Serenity by the Sea

A crab wore a hat, quite absurd,
Each wave made him dance, quite absurd,
Seagulls cawed jokes at the pier,
While fish flipped their tails with cheer.

A sandcastle stood, proud and grand,
Until the tide rolled in, unplanned,
It waved goodbye with a splashy schmooze,
While kids just laughed in their soggy shoes.

Echoes of Distant Horizons

A dolphin with swagger, strutted by,
He winked at a fish as it swam by,
Their giggles echoed across the sea,
As crabs climbed rocks, laughing with glee.

Each wave whispered jokes to the shore,
While surfers just tumbled, craving more,
The sun slipped down, a slippery drip,
As mermaids giggled on every trip.

The Dance of Light on Water

A fish in sunglasses swam with pride,
While turtles raced, but mostly just glide,
The sunbulb shimmered, spun like a top,
As jellyfish floated, in cosmic bop.

At dusk, the tide threw a wild ball,
Seashells rolled over, laughing for all,
Each splash was a punchline, dearly spun,
While crabs did the moonwalk, just for fun.

Tranquil Reflections

A beach ball bounced with a silly grin,
While smoothies spilled free, and laughter skimmed,
The sun dipped low, a flirtatious tease,
As sandcastles chuckled in the evening breeze.

The tide tickled toes in a playful race,
While seaweed danced, in a green embrace,
Fish leapt high, telling tales of the day,
As shadows whispered secrets, fading away.

Dance of the Seafoam

The waves do a wiggly dance,
Each splash a silly chance.
Seafoam giggles, tides collide,
In this frothy, joyful ride.

Seagulls dive in awkward flights,
Chasing fish with all their might.
Water tickles toes in glee,
While crabs perform their crabby spree.

Buckets spill, oh what a mess!
Sandcastles teeter, more or less.
With every wave, a splashy fate,
Who knew the ocean could be so great?

A beach ball boinks with cheerful sound,
As sunbathers lounge all around.
A dog runs in with stick in tow,
Pretending it's a pro, you know!

The Luster of New Beginnings

A fresh day dawns with a wink,
Bright toes in water, let's not sink!
Flip-flops flying, laughter spills,
As everyone escapes the drills.

Seashells giggle as they chat,
"Look at this one, isn't that fat?"
In the sand, a treasure hunt,
Finding smiles, that's the fun front.

Kites dance high, flapping with pride,
While sunburnt folks try to hide.
Each wave brings a brand-new joke,
As the tide swirls and folks provoke.

New friends made with each splash,
Silly stories, oh what a bash!
With ice cream dripping down your hand,
Life is sweet on this sunny land.

A Day's First Light

Morning breaks with a giggly glow,
Beach towels tossed in a hefty row.
Coffee spills, oh what a sight,
As seagulls squawk just for spite!

Children race with squeals of jest,
While parents claim a morning rest.
A crab plays hide-and-seek in shells,
While sandcastles sound their ringing bells.

Joggers trip on the smooth, soft grain,
Only to roll and start again!
The ocean waves play peekaboo,
Promising fun with skies so blue.

Barefoot dancing, splashes everywhere,
With salty winds, tousled hair.
A day unfolds in playful spree,
Life's too short, let's just be free!

A Canvas of Waves

The ocean paints with foamy strokes,
Brush of sunlight, laughter provokes.
Each ripple tells a joke so grand,
While crabs strut like they own the sand.

Surfboards crash, then ride the swell,
Falling flat, oh can't you tell?
In the water, splashes erupt,
As swimmers find the joy corrupt!

A child builds a tower of shells,
In the wind, it almost yells.
Jellyfish dangle, come take a look,
They flop along like a funny book!

With laughter echoing down the shore,
Footprints follow where giggles roar.
This canvas of joy is where we play,
At the beach, we'll never sway!

Tidal Shimmer

Waves dance and shimmy, oh what a sight,
Seagulls squawk loudly, they're quite the fright.
Sandcastles topple as kids make a scene,
Laughter erupts, everyone's a teen.

Buckets and shovels are scattered with glee,
Who's building what? Oh, not me, not me!
A beach ball flies, a dog joins the fun,
Round and round chasing, until they are done.

Ice cream drips down and stains little shirts,
Sticky-faced children, oh how it hurts!
But watch as they giggle, trip over a shoe,
Falling like heroes, they'll start over, too!

As twilight whispers, the fun's not quite through,
With fireflies dancing and stars breaking through.
They'll tell ghostly tales, though they're not too scary,
Just kids and the crabs, oh, how they are merry!

Mosaic of Dawn

Morning's a mess with bright colors galore,
Bikini mishaps leave everyone sore.
The coffee's too hot and the toast's burnt as well,
But laughter's the recipe that we know so well.

Flip-flops a-flop, they go left, then to right,
Tripping over sunbeams, oh what a sight!
The seagulls are squawking a morning song,
With everyone singing, can't none go wrong!

Parrots are gossiping, oh, what a tease!
They spill all the secrets, with elegant ease.
A crab struts by with an attitude boast,
You'd think he's the king, with his pinchy little post.

As shadows grow longer, the fun's still alive,
We dance like we're crazy, just glad to survive.
With laughter the wave that we all ride upon,
This goofy mosaic is never too gone!

Amber Tides

At dawn the sand glows, like butter, quite bright,
While seagulls play tag, taking flight in delight.
Oops! There goes my sandwich, a swift thrifty take!
Now they have my lunch and my heart starts to ache.

Two kids make a splash, splash goes the drink,
Giggles abound, and the grown-ups just blink.
Who's getting wet next? It's all up to chance!
Oh look, the old man! He's doing a dance!

The sun plays peek-a-boo with clouds so fluffy,
While a dog digs a hole, his nose all puffy.
They say he's a hero; he finds a lost shoe,
But all he seeks, really, is that treat for two!

As sun bows to evening, with colors ablaze,
We gather round to share our funniest phase.
And with flickering lights, we'll tell tales so grand,
While the waves clap their hands, oh isn't life grand?

Rays of Joy

Start the day with pancakes, as syrup takes flight,
Little hands reach out, "Just one more bite!"
The beach is a circus, with clowns by the shore,
Juggling beach balls, oh, what a galore!

Time for a swim, but the tide says, "No!"
As kids make a splash, while adults say "Whoa!"
Someone's lost a flip-flop, it floats like a star,
The search for the lost shoe? It's traveled too far!

Seashells are treasures, or so they all say,
But they're just fancy rocks, in a kid's fray.
"Found a rare gem!" one kid shouts with pride,
"It's just a piece of seaweed, but let's not abide."

As evening approaches, and sky turns to gold,
There's laughter and stories, adventures retold.
With rays of pure joy, our hearts intertwine,
Making memories together like a fine vintage wine.

Awash in Warmth

The seagulls squawk with a quirk,
While beach balls bounce in the murk.
Sunscreen's splatter, sticky and bright,
Mixes with laughter, oh what a sight!

Children chase waves with glee,
One trips, adds to the comedy.
Sandcastles topple, not quite supreme,
But who cares? It's all part of the dream!

Tanning lotion, a slippery mess,
One slip, and everyone's in distress.
Flip-flops flapping, a stylish feat,
Oh look! Someone's lost a shoe on the street!

As we sip drinks, there's quite a spill,
Hey, is that a crab with a will?
With goofy grins, we toast the day,
At this sandy spot, come what may!

A Symphony of Aquatic Colors

Fins flapping, fish parade with flair,
Colors clash like a wild hair.
Under the waves, a party's grand,
Jellyfish bobbing, look at them stand!

Octopus juggling shells with ease,
While turtles glide like ocean breeze.
They all dance in a wavy trance,
It's a slapstick, not a solemn chance!

Coral reefs are a vibrant stage,
Where clownfish act like they're on a page.
Each little critter plays their role,
In this nautical sitcom, they stroll!

Even the seaweed's doing the cha-cha,
As crabs slide by, waving 'hola'.
Nature laughs in aquatic rhyme,
Making waves—it's a splashy time!

Secrets of the Salty Breeze

The salty wind whispers tales so sly,
Of seagulls in sunglasses, oh my!
They strut like stars on this beachy stage,
With humor and grace, they steal every page.

Footprints in sand, but look out below,
Where one slips, a wet face will show!
Towels become sails in a gusty spree,
As laughter erupts with every degree.

Kites fly high, caught in a loop,
While kids build a fort, just for the scoop.
A wave crashes down, and oh, what a sight!
The splash hits an elder—talk about fright!

Gossip spreads like the tide on the shore,
"Did you see that?" Oh, who could ignore?
With every breeze, stories are spun,
Life's a riot when you're having fun!

Where the Light Meets the Depths

Sunbeams glint in the water's dance,
Where fish flirt and take a chance.
Bubbles rise like giggles in play,
They bob and weave, chasing today.

Surfboards bob with youthful zest,
A wipeout here? Just part of the jest.
Splash fights emerge, no rules at hand,
As laughter echoes across the sand.

Mermaids sing in silly tones,
While dolphins jump like light-hearted clowns.
Underwater, it's a wacky team,
In this watery world, who needs a dream?

The day melts into a funny glow,
As shadows stretch and laughter flows.
Each wave brings tales so absurd,
In this realm, giggles are the word!

The Awakening Coast

Waves whisper secrets to the sand,
Seagulls gossip, all quite grand.
Shells with gossip, tales to share,
I found a crab that just won't care.

Tides are rolling, drinks in hand,
Flip-flops flying, isn't it grand?
Sunscreen smudged on everyone's nose,
We laugh till the sun starts to doze.

Here comes the ocean, full of cheer,
Oh no! Here comes a bouncing deer!
Chasing waves with a silly dance,
Watch out for the seagull's prance!

Picnics messy with splattered fries,
And soda rockets make us all cry.
We slip and slide with joyful grins,
Sandy snacks sneak into our chins.

Brightness Beyond the Blue

Dolphins dance on their bright, shiny backs,
Tickling toes as we laugh at the hacks.
Colors splash in the playful spree,
Sips of juice, sticky as can be.

The beachball bounces, oh, what a sight,
It hits a mom, and giggles ignite!
Kites twirl high in the airy dome,
Catching a breeze, they're calling us home.

Sandcastles rise, but soon they will fall,
A sponge cake towers; we'll eat it all.
Ants on a mission, they march in a line,
Why do they think crumbs taste so divine?

A sunburned nose, a splashy good time,
We're singing old songs, every last rhyme.
The waves are loud, they cheer us along,
We're just silly, where we all belong.

Chronicles of Light and Tide

Once upon a wave, far from the shore,
A fish told jokes, we begged for more.
He flipped through the air with a glorious splash,
Lured in a crab for a wiggly bash.

Sandwiches flying like birds on a spree,
Lettuce made hats for the kids by the sea.
Beach towels tangled in a sunset glow,
Who knew that sunburn would make us all glow?

Flip-flops skid like rollerblades clad,
Falling like dominoes, oh, isn't that sad?
A parade of seaweed, our costume delight,
Onlookers chuckle, what a funny sight!

Seashells as trophies for pier-side games,
Thumb wrested with fish, they play for the names.
Then night takes the shore, with giggles in tow,
We dream of the ocean and the morning's glow.

Daylight Dreams by the Sea

Balloons afloat like jellyfish pop,
Laughter bounces, we hop, hop, hop.
Picnics of pickle, a saltwater spree,
Sand toys scatter, they all want to flee.

In the coolness, we surprise each other,
That splash was a fish or a giggling brother?
Chasing the tide, oh, what fun it'll be,
As flip-flops squelch in mirth by the spree.

Silly seashells whisper tales from the deep,
Mermaids giggle; they just can't keep.
Cuddly crabs with their claw on the go,
Sanding the beach with dramatic show.

As daylight fades, our voices sing clear,
Who knew laughter could echo so near?
The sea, our canvas, our laughter, our call,
Daylight dreams keep us laughing through it all.

Glistening Sands

On the beach, my toes did dig,
Losing my flip-flops, oh what a gig!
Seagulls swoop down for a snack,
While I'm just trying to get my back.

The waves come in, they crash and tease,
Saltwater hair and a sticky breeze.
I tried to build, a castle tall,
But ended up splashing—oh take that fall!

Sunburned nose and silly shades,
Grabbing ice cream, hopes it cascades.
I slip on a wave and do a twirl,
End up soaked, oh what a whirl!

As the tide rolls out, I chase my hat,
And wonder if seagulls think I'm fat.
We laugh and dance on this sandy floor,
Making memories, who could ask for more?

Horizon's Promenade

Strolling the boardwalk with ice cream in hand,
Seagull conspiracies we do demand.
Footprints in sand, a zig-zag line,
"Are we drunk on sun or just feeling fine?"

Rides and games, I shout, "I'll win!"
Toss a ring—and I miss again!
The laughter erupts as I trip on my shoe,
A comic relief for my friends, it's true!

Sandcastle competition, we take our stand,
With moats and towers made by hand.
Judges are seagulls, perched on the wall,
Who knew that birds could taunt us all?

As evening falls and colors expand,
We spot a dolphin, both cute and grand.
We wave at the splash, "You're the real star!"
Dolphin responds with a splash from afar!

Dreams in the Foam

Kicking at foam as it swirls around,
In my daydreams, a mermaid I found.
"Can I join you?" I ask with a grin,
She just bubbles and rolls back in.

Crabs in coats dancing a crabby jig,
On the shoreline, they strut quite big.
"Hey, watch this!" I shout with glee,
But tumble right down—oh, woe is me!

Shells whisper secrets, or so I think,
But mostly, they smell like a fishy stink.
This seaweed hat is surely a win,
Until the tide says, "Oh, that's been!"

As day fades, stars pop like laughter,
And I wonder what comes after this chapter.
Floating on dreams, with foam as my sail,
Summers are sweet, with whimsical tales!

Laughter on the Breeze

The breeze carries giggles, oh what a sound,
As my beach umbrella flops to the ground.
I chase it down, looking quite the mess,
"Was this a good idea?" I still just guess.

Playing frisbee turns into a fight,
As it lands in the cooler, oh what a sight!
Soda sprays high, a fizzy delight,
We all burst out laughing—oh, what a night!

The bonfire crackles, we roast marshmallows,
"More chocolate!" someone loudly bellows.
But the s'mores become gooey, stuck on my face,
An edible mask—oh, what a disgrace!

As stars twinkle down, we all share a cheer,
With stories of mishaps, we hold each dear.
Life's a beach, they say, so soak in the glee,
With laughter on breezes, forever carefree!

Golden Tides

The beach ball bounced, quite out of hand,
It landed in the ice cream stand.
A seagull swiped a cone with glee,
While kids squealed loud, "That's not for me!"

A crab wore shades, looking quite cool,
While the waves danced, splashing the pool.
A sunburnt dad, in a chair, snores,
Dreaming of fish and endless shores.

Footprints traced in sand like a map,
Leading to snacks, then a quick nap.
The tide rolled in with a playful tease,
Tickling toes with the softest breeze.

The ice cream's melting, what a sight!
Chasing the seagulls, oh what a fright!
With laughter loud, the day drifts by,
Under the watchful, laughing sky.

Whispering Waves

The waves whispered jokes, oh so clever,
About a turtle who swims forever.
A dolphin danced, making a splash,
While beachgoers laughed, what a bash!

Finding shells, the treasure of the day,
But one giggled back, "Hey, put me away!"
A fish in disguise tried to hitch a ride,
While crabs wore hats—such fun, they couldn't hide.

A kid brings a bucket, but it's upside down,
Holding sand that looks like a crown.
"Look, I'm royalty!" he sings with zest,
While seagulls plot, "Let's put him to the test!"

Surfboards crashing, they ride a wave,
To the rhythm of the ocean's rave.
With laughter echoing through the air,
These moments cherished, beyond compare.

Dawn's Embrace

The morning sun peeked, with a yawn,
As surfers stretched, all sleepy and drawn.
A seagull called, "Do you smell that bread?"
While a kid spilled juice all over his head.

The sandcastle towers, wobbly and grand,
Built by kids with snacks in hand.
"Moat's made of jelly!" one proudly shouts,
While a wave says, "Not for long, watch out!"

Paddling out, a dog joins the fun,
Chasing sticks, thinking he's number one.
With cartwheels and laughter beneath the sun,
This goofy crew knows how to run.

The tide rolls in, taking all bets,
But the joy remains, with no regrets.
Sand on their toes, smiles so bright,
This silly day feels just right!

Beneath the Radiant Skies

Beneath the blue where the clouds dance high,
A kid chased rainbows, a gleam in his eye.
His bucket hat, as bright as the day,
Said, "Catch those colors!" in a funny way.

A starfish waved, not wanting to stay,
Screaming "Beach party!" in its own quirky way.
With flip-flops flopping and sunburned backs,
They all fell flat with laughter, no lack!

An octopus in shades played DJ on sand,
Spinning seashells to a wild band.
With jellyfish doing the latest dance,
Everyone joined in, a wacky prance!

As the sun dipped low, painting the night,
With giggles and stories, hearts felt so light.
Under the stars, they couldn't dismiss,
The magic of laughter that none could miss.

The Reflection of Being

Bobbing heads and sunburned toes,
Chasing seagulls who steal your nose.
Umbrella battles, a fierce sand fight,
Crabs in the cooler, what a delight!

Flip-flops flying through the salty air,
Someone's gone rogue, what a sweet dare!
Laughter erupts with a splash and a squeal,
Sunscreen fails, but oh, what a deal!

Waves in a Golden Embrace

The waves waltz in a dancing spree,
Knocking umbrellas down, wild and free.
Fish take cover; they laugh in glee,
While children erupt in a 'wet T-shirt' decree!

Sandy sandwiches, a seagull feast,
You microwave chips, what a treat released!
High tide waits for no one's charm,
Quick! Grab the cooler, or else... it's harmed!

Where Sky Meets the Water

With skies so blue and clouds like cheese,
A man in shorts is stung by a breeze.
He jumps and runs, a fantastic show,
Like a fish caught trying to steal a toe!

Surfboards topple like clumsy friends,
As tides tickle toes and laughter blends.
Every splash writes a story anew,
As sunscreen sprays like confetti, woohoo!

Vistas of Buffed Bronze

Muscles flex in a pose so grand,
But the towel slips—oh, wasn't it planned?
Rubber ducks audition for a new role,
As waves whisper secrets to every soul.

Barefoot antics, the sand feels right,
Someone drops ice cream, what a sad sight!
But look—a treasure! A pirate's prize,
It's only a flip-flop, oh, how time flies!

Golden Memories at Water's Edge

Seagulls dance on the breeze,
Chasing chips with such ease.
Fishermen with bait in hand,
Hoping for fish, not just sand.

Kids build castles with flair,
While dogs dig without a care.
Ice cream drips down my wrist,
Sweet treats I can't resist.

The lifeguard snores on the chair,
While a crab creeps by with a stare.
A picnic blanket finds a way,
To become a bird's buffet.

Time slips away, oh what a sight,
Laughter echoes into the night.
With golden rays all around,
These silly moments, joy abound.

Embraced by Ocean's Caress

Waves tickle toes and squeals arise,
As salty water meets the skies.
Flipping flip-flops all around,
Lost one? Better look, it's drowned!

Sandy hair, a bird's new nest,
Parents sigh, hoping for rest.
Someone yells, 'Watch where you throw!'
A frisbee flies, where'd it go?

The beach ball's flown, it took a dive,
But watch that kid, he's so alive!
Splashing through puddles with glee,
Creating waves, as wild as can be.

Sunsets bring a golden hue,
As laughter lingers, bright and true.
They say the water's just for fun,
But I think it's where all mischief's spun.

The Magic of Sandy Footprints

Tiny footprints jammed in sand,
Leading to where sea meets land.
Shells collected, oh such weight,
Who knew treasure could be a plate?

A crab scuttles, gives a fright,
While I'm laughing with delight.
Chasing waves as they retreat,
Dancing back, oh what a feat!

Sandy sandwiches, a bold design,
With beach bugs adding a tasty line.
Who knew lunch could be so fun?
With grains of sand, we might weigh a ton!

Sunsets glow, our shadows grow,
As evening calls, we'll let it flow.
With every step, the beach we chase,
Crafting memories we can embrace.

Journey to the Lighted Shore

The path to laughter all aglow,
Where wild beach dances, oh what a show!
With friends in tow, we roam and roam,
Each wave brings tales we can call home.

Shell finds its way into my shoe,
Found surprises, who knew, who knew?
Waves crash loud with a giggle spree,
Echoed by the joy of you and me.

Starfish and jelly, quite a pair,
Dancing gently through salty air.
While seagulls plot their next great heist,
We arm ourselves with chips, oh how nice!

As the sun dips lower in the sky,
A funny wind whispers, oh my, oh my!
With laughter ringing, fun in store,
Our journey here, forevermore.

Dreams on the Ocean's Edge

Seagulls squawk, a cheeky crew,
Stealing fries from folks like you.
A crab does the cha-cha on the sand,
While tourists pose like they're so grand.

Waves roll in, they tickle toes,
But splashes come, and laughter flows.
Beach balls bounce, a slippery race,
Someone's hat—now, it's gone with grace!

Sunscreen fights and slipping slides,
Kids run wild like they're on rides.
The ice cream truck rolls into sight,
A chase ensues—now that's a fright!

With sandcastles standing proud and tall,
Pails and shovels—let's have a ball!
While crabs plot hedges, they conspire,
To steal our picnic—oh, I admire!

A Symphony of Light

Under umbrellas, sun hats gleam,
An orchestra of laughter and ice cream.
Children's giggles, a bright refrain,
As waves clap hands, a crazy gain!

Flip-flops flapping, a lively tune,
While sand ticks dance like a cartoon.
A sunburnt lobster, red as can be,
Wonders why he's the joke of the sea!

Seashells whisper shady tales,
Of the brave crabs and their tiny gales.
Dancing mermaids, oh so bold,
In their seaweed crowns and glittering gold.

The lifeguard sleeps, with a casual flair,
Dreaming of dolphins and jellyfish air.
Waves take a bow, the day is bright,
In this wacky symphony, everything's light.

Melodies of the Shore

The sandy beach plays a silly tune,
As flip-flops squeak 'neath a sunny moon.
A fish in a bucket swims with glee,
While a dog rolls over like it's free!

Towels tangled, a colorful mess,
Someone's lost, but who's to confess?
Umbrellas flutter, a wind caught prize,
As seagulls circle with keen, quick eyes.

Beachgoers laugh, they dodge and dive,
One slips on a jellyfish—oh, what a jive!
Kites in the air, a bright, bold dance,
As beachballs bounce, they take their chance.

A conch shell blown, but what's that sound?
A dog requesting snacks all around.
When the day wraps with a sunburned score,
We pack up memories from the shore!

Celestial Pathways

On the shore, where the sun rays play,
Sandcastles bloom, then wash away.
A crab prances like it's in a show,
While kids throw water, just for the glow!

Kites soaring high, dancing with breeze,
Waves whisper secrets, teasing our knees.
An ice cream spill, laughter erupts,
As a friendly pouf of cotton candy disrupts.

Shells with stories lie everywhere,
While dolphins peek, as if they care.
Tanning toasts, as the sun sets low,
We stumble and tumble—what a great show!

Stars twinkle up in the vast night sky,
Reflecting dreams of laughter gone by.
As crickets sing their coastal song,
We drift homeward, feeling so strong!

Echoes of Radiance

On sandy dunes, I lost my shoe,
The seagulls laughed, as they flew too.
A crab danced by, in a funky groove,
I joined the show, trying to move.

A beach ball soared, hit a sunbather,
His snacks flew high, oh, what a wager!
Laughter erupted, the tide came in,
We played it cool, hiding our grin.

Umbrella flopped, gave us a scare,
My lemonade spilled, I sat in despair.
But splashes of joy filled the air,
As we rolled on sand, without a care.

The waves tickled toes, we laughed and shrieked,
Every sea foam story has its peak.
With salty hair and sunburned nose,
We named the crabs, let our fun expose.

Sunkissed Whispers

Flip-flops squeaking, we're all a mess,
Chasing waves, a sandy caress.
Someone tripped, fell on their rear,
Caught in a splash, yet grinning ear to ear.

Ice cream cones melted in the sun,
Sticky fingers, oh, what fun!
Seagulls plotting, swoops in the sky,
Dodging their dive, oh my, oh my!

Tanning lotion, a slippery quest,
Turned my belly into a shiny crest.
Trying to roll, I got stuck,
Laughter erupted, oh, what luck!

With every wave, our worries drift,
Sandcastles built, like a fun gift.
We'll nap under towels, dream aloud,
On this beach, we're lost in a crowd.

Timeless Glows

The sunbeams play, casting a spell,
I lost my hat, oh, what the hell!
It flew like a bird, up high it soared,
Chased by laughter, we all adored.

Giggling kids, with buckets in hand,
Building castles, a whimsical land.
Yet the waves rolled in, with mischief abound,
Towers fell down, with a splashing sound.

My friend slipped, did a spectacular dive,
Into a puddle, oh, he came alive!
Sand stuck everywhere, even in his nose,
Our giggles erupted, joy overflows.

Evening comes, draped in gold,
Stories exchanged, memories told.
With salty hugs and laughter's glow,
We danced through time, hearts all aglow.

The Beauty of Morning Tides

Morning breaks with a cheeky grin,
Coffee spills, oh where to begin?
Waves whisper secrets, quick to tease,
As beachgoers dance in a silly breeze.

Seagulls squawk, like they know it all,
Diving for snacks, an early call.
Catch and release, but I missed that throw,
Half a sandwich, now they steal the show.

Sandy treasures, flip-flops askew,
Spying on crabs who look stuck too.
My friend got pranked, covered in seaweed,
Rolling in laughter, a true friend indeed!

The tides retreat, calling us near,
We chase after waves, let go of fear.
With every splash, all worries fade,
Beach day silliness, perfectly played.

Kaleidoscope of Light

Waves flip-flop with a splashy sound,
Seagulls gossip, spinning 'round.
Sandcastles lean with a lopsided flair,
While beachgoers play like they haven't a care.

Kids chase crabs with a squeaky glee,
While sunscreen flies like confetti, you see.
A giant beach ball rolls off the sand,
Colliding with sunbathers, oh isn't it grand?

Flip-flops flutter like butterflies bright,
Everyone's dancing in the warm, golden light.
The lifeguard snoozes with a haphazard grin,
As tourists try surfing, their chances are thin!

But laughter cascades like the waves that do crash,
Every moment here feels like a bash.
So grab your umbrella and a fruity drink,
Life's too funny not to stop and wink!

Glistening Shores of Promise

Towels unroll like a bright colored map,
Fried food wafts, oh what a trap!
Sandy toes have a mind of their own,
And shells whisper secrets when we're alone.

Ice cream drips down like a melted dream,
While tourists try catching a seagull's gleam.
Skimpy swimsuits might cause a scare,
As onlookers giggle, some simply stare.

Boys build weird shapes, all wobbly and tall,
While girls gossip brightly, ready to haul.
The sun takes a selfie, shedding its rays,
And flip-flop fashion becomes the next craze!

But as fun unfolds on this bright, sunny strip,
The best memories come from the odd little trip.
Bubbles in the air, laughter so loud,
Who knew the beach could be such a crowd?

The Horizon's Glow

Waves leap and dance like rubber band kids,
While sunscreen missile misfires and skids.
Beach umbrellas pop up like mushrooms in bloom,
Creating a picnic place full of room.

Sun hats spin in a windstorm of cheer,
As everyone's mixed up, where's that last beer?
A crab steals a chip and scuttles away,
While the lifeguard's imitation puts others at bay.

Fishing poles become javelins from the surf,
Who would've thought? They're better than turf!
Seagull symphonies sing sweet, silly tunes,
As sunbathing buddies get baked like balloons.

With laughter like waves rushing back to the shore,
Each moment here feels like forever more.
So cruise on the fun, let joy overflow,
In the heart of this place where the summer winds blow!

Serenity in Rays

Picnics set sail with bizarre little snacks,
While ants plot a heist to steal all the packs!
Beach volleyball bounces, a glorious mess,
As players duck, weave, and curse in distress.

The tide rolls in like a playful dog,
Waves lap at toes, it's a splashy fog.
Some folks are graceful, others just splash,
As swimsuits seem destined for an epic crash.

Moms yell at kids who've wandered too deep,
While dads pose cool, trying not to sleep.
A rescue float drifts with a life of its own,
As comedians emerge from the sand like a drone.

Laughter erupts while the sun starts to dip,
And the tales of the day become one long trip.
So let's share a smile, raise a toast to the sun,
Life's too short not to laugh, let's have some fun!

The Breath of Day

Woke up to a banana peel,
Slipped on my way to the meal.
Coffee's brewing, oh what a sight,
It splashed everywhere, what a fright!

Birds are chirping, they won't stop,
One just landed on my mop.
Thought I'd swim in the morning dew,
But found a puddle, oh no, boo-hoo!

Sun's peeking in, all so bright,
My toaster's dancing with delight.
Tropics calling, come take a trip,
Just keep your shoes, hold on to your lip!

I'll take my hat, go on a spree,
With socks that clash, oh woe is me!
Flip-flops flapping on my feet,
Dancing past the dog, what a treat!

Glorious Morning Crests

Rise and shine, my toast is stuck,
I pried it free, oh what a muck.
The cat looks on with judgment clear,
While I just laugh and grab a beer!

The waves they crash, oh what a show,
A seagull swoops, a feathered foe.
He snatches fries from my plate divine,
"Hey buddy, those are totally mine!"

Sand between toes, grains in my hat,
A crab is scheming, what a brat!
He pinched my lunch, scuttled away,
I chased him down, oh what a day!

Blessed with sun and goofy vibes,
All around, the laughter jibes.
We'll dance on sand, forget the stress,
In flip-flops, who needs to impress?

Glistening Shores of Tranquility

My beach ball's popped, oh what a shock,
It made a noise like an angry rock.
Inflated dreams now just a mess,
But the beach puns? They're anyone's guess!

The tide rolls in, a wave of fun,
A toddler shrieks, "We're on the run!"
A dolphin jumps with perfect timing,
While I'm just here, semi-climbing!

Sandcastles built with grand designs,
Before the wave dines on our lines.
Next time I'll build with moats, I swear,
Forget the towers, we'll bring a bear!

Laughing hard under the sun,
Trip over sand, oh what a run!
No worries here, just silly plays,
On a beach that sings through sunny days!

Whispers Beneath Blue Skies

Beneath the sky, a kite in flight,
It took a turn, oh what a sight!
Tangled in my hat, it gives a shout,
"Free me now, I want to scout!"

Sunburned nose, I'm feeling grand,
Spotting dolphins, sand in hand.
But wait! My friend just lost a drink,
Splashed by waves, we laugh and wink.

Picnic spread, but ants declare,
"Come join us, we have snacks to share!"
I gave a cheer, and they all came,
My sandwich gone, but what a game!

With playful breezes swirling near,
A day of fun, that's crystal clear.
So flip those towels, let laughter fly,
Underneath the vast and sunny sky!

Coastal Reflections

Seagulls squawk, a silly chatter,
As crabs do their dance, with splashes that splatter.
The beach ball flies, with a comical flair,
While sunscreen's applied, but misses the hair.

Buckets are stacked, like a tower of dreams,
But down they all tumble, or so it seems.
Children giggle, as waves crash around,
Then a tumbleweed rolls, is that lost and found?

Sandcastles built with great pride and with haste,
Only to crumble like whipped cream on paste.
Wave after wave, the tide's funny game,
Leaves us with laughter, and no one to blame.

As the sun dips low, a grand farewell sight,
We frolic and tumble, making memories bright.
With smiles and with giggles, we dance to the shore,
Until the next wave calls, who could want more?

The Horizon's Touch

The horizon dances, with shades so bizarre,
Waving to surfers who swipe like a car.
With boogie boards flying, the splashiest show,
Lifeguards keep laughing, just watching the flow.

Beach umbrellas flipping, they sail like a boat,
While a cat on a leash tries to stay afloat.
Fishermen's tales grow taller each day,
'Twas a whale! No, a fish! That got away!

The sand's full of treasures, just look and you'll see,
A flip-flop, a shell, and a jellyfish spree.
Everyone's chasing the ice cream truck's song,
But when it runs out... that's where we go wrong!

At dusk when the colors make all of us sigh,
We caper and chuckle under the vast sky.
With each silly moment, as time rolls in fast,
We laugh in the present, forgetting the past.

A Serenade to the Sun

Oh, Mr. Sun, with your golden smile,
Your warmth is so charming, let's linger a while.
We dance in the heat, our feet in the sand,
I dropped my cold drink! Isn't that just grand?

Beach chairs recline, some tilt with the breeze,
While a toddler demands, "More squirt guns, please!"
A frisbee flies high, and a dog gives a chase,
Wagging his tail, and now he's lost pace.

The rhythm grows louder, as music will play,
But one song's so catchy, it keeps us at bay.
Flip-flops in hand, we sway to the beat,
While someone trips over their own two left feet!

As sunset arrives, we gather in glee,
For laughter's our language—can you hear it, see?
With a toast of cool drinks, we raise them up high,
To the funny little moments that make laughter fly!

Streams of Sunshine

In pools filled with giggles and splashes around,
Water fights break out, with laughter profound.
Rubber duck races, it's a serious sport,
While moms keep on shouting, "Keep it all short!"

The tanned sunbathers lay slack on their towels,
While kids with their buckets act just like owls.
Under bright umbrellas, the gossip runs wild,
About beach tales of silly, they leave us all riled!

With kites in the sky, they dance up so high,
One tangles in hair, with a sigh and a cry.
But every mishap just heightens the fun,
Who knew that a breezy day could weigh a ton?

As stars start to twinkle, the day bids goodbye,
With stories retold under a glowing sky.
With memories crafted, the fun can't be pressed,
We'll laugh here again, with the sun as our guest!

The Harmony of Tides and Light

Seagulls dance and caw with glee,
Their shadows race, wild and free.
A crab in disguise, with a slow, sly crawl,
Wears a beach hat, looking oh-so-small.

Children giggle, building their dreams,
While ice cream drips down their sun-kissed beams.
A wave crashes, with laughter it blends,
As someone shouts, 'Watch out for bends!'

A sandcastle throne made with care,
Where a rubber duck presides, full of flair.
The tide rolls back, giving a sigh,
As the duck takes flight, oh me, oh my!

With flip-flops flying, we run and we laugh,
Chasing the surf, oh what a gaffe!
The ocean's a prankster, playful and bright,
Who knew the sea could have such insight?

Golden Waves of Morning

At dawn, it's all fish and chips,
As seagulls dive for morning dips.
A sunbeam winks at old driftwood,
Whispering 'dance', in a language misunderstood.

Sandcastles crumble with style and flair,
As kids fly by on a donut chair.
A dolphin hops, with a laugh so grand,
Is it just me, or he's got a band?

Buckets and shovels, oh what a crew,
Digging for treasures, or just for some goo!
A sand-sculpture of dad, looking so bold,
Collapses with giggles, or so I'm told.

Mismatched socks on sun-kissed feet,
Stumbling together, oh what a feat!
With laughter that sparkles as bright as the sun,
We frolic and play—oh, life is just fun!

Radiance by the Sea

A crab in a bowtie sways to a beat,
While sipping his drink, quite the cool treat.
A sunbather snorts, as waves come with force,
And splashes are met with an "Oh my, of course!"

Jellyfish float like balloons in the air,
While sandcastles stand, preparing to dare.
A dog steals a frisbee, with a playful bark,
As its owner dives in, landing quite stark!

Seashells gossip, oh the tales they weave,
Of mermaids with hair that boys won't believe.
A seagull swoops to grab a pretzel, so bold,
"Hey, buddy, that's mine!" it seems to scold.

A sunset parade of vibrant hues,
That tickles the sky, like a painter's muse.
With laughter and joy, we dance on the sand,
Oh the stories we'll tell, remember this band!

Embrace of the Dawn

The sun peeks out with a goofy grin,
As the first wave crashes, ushering in.
A snorkeler fumbles with gear gone rogue,
As seaweed tangles, in a not-so-cool vogue.

Waves chuckle softly, secrets they hold,
Of surfers who wobbled, and brightly colored gold.
With flip-flops slapping, they dash to the sea,
Creating a ruckus, wild and carefree.

Kites fly high, like laughter on strings,
While crabs hold a party, wearing bling rings.
Parents shout, "No running!" as chaos ensues,
But their ice cream cone? That's their daily news!

The end of the day, with skies painted pink,
Together we sit, and share a good wink.
In this funny ballet, where joy is the theme,
Life's an adventure, a whimsical dream!

Dancing Dunes

The sand took on a wiggly groove,
As waves whispered secrets it couldn't prove.
A crab in a tutu threw quite the dance,
While seagulls laughed at their silly prance.

The sun gave high-fives to the sandy hills,
As beach balls bounced, igniting the thrills.
A flip-flop flew, aimed straight for a hat,
While a seagull grinned, 'Oh, now that's where it's at!'

The dunes all giggled, catching the breeze,
As surfers rode in like kings on their knees.
But alas! A tumble, a slip, and a roll,
Made it a day where laughter took toll.

At twilight's curtain, the dunes yawned wide,
Inviting the stars for a rollercoaster ride.
So next time you visit, just follow the fun,
For the dunes are alive—though they're not on the run!

Melodies of the Coastal Whisper

Waves humming tunes like a sweet lullaby,
As shells held concerts for the gulls in the sky.
A dolphin choreographed an aquatic ballet,
While fish clapped lightly, cheering on the display.

A crab played the drums on a coconut shell,
And sandy beachgoers danced oh-so-well.
Flip-flops clicked like castanets in the sun,
As the tides swayed back, inviting more fun.

The lighthouse spun lights that sang out of tune,
While starfish strummed guitars beneath the moon.
The sea breeze chimed in with the finest refrain,
Making the ocean seem funny and plain insane!

So if you ever feel caught in a whir,
Just come seek the melodies, let your heart stir.
For the coast holds a symphony of gleeful delight,
With humor wrapped all 'round, making everything right.

Rays of Hope at Sunset

The sun slipped down like a banana peel,
And jellyfish floated, oh what a deal!
While surfers grinned, catching the last wave,
A whale blew a bubble, ever so brave.

Seagulls planned dinner, a fishy buffet,
While a clam rolled its eyes, in a grumpy display.
The ocean turned orange, like a giant fruit pie,
With laughter erupting, as crabs started to fly.

Beach towels tangled, forming a nest,
While kids chased shadows, never at rest.
A sunset so silly, it tickled the sky,
As the sand cast giggles, oh me, oh my!

As stars popped open, like fizzy drinks,
The waves whispered secrets, what the moon thinks.
So chase the horizon, let worries take flight,
For dusk brings the joy of a playful twilight.

A Warm Embrace Among Waves

The sea hugged the sand with a frothy delight,
As beach bears rolled in under pure moonlight.
A walrus in shades struck a pose for a pic,
While dolphins retorted with tricks oh-so-quick.

Sunbathers flipped like pancakes on grills,
And sunscreen fights erupted with shrills.
A starfish proposed to a mermaid so fair,
While sea turtles laughed at the spectacle there!

Beach umbrellas danced, blown by the winds,
While towels sang songs like forgotten old friends.
The laughter of children filled up the air,
As waves made confetti from sand without care.

So join in the meek, in the waves' warm embrace,
And let go of worries, come dance with the grace.
For every splash tells a joke, bright and free,
Making moments of joy as easy as can be!

Marigold Memories

In flip-flops I took a grand stroll,
Toward a beach that was far from my goal.
Seagulls squawked with glee, quite absurd,
I dropped my ice cream, oh how it blurred.

My towel flew high, oh what a sight,
It danced o'er the waves, a true kite flight.
Kids giggled as I chased it round,
That silly towel, so much joy I found.

Sandcastles crumbled, a royal mess,
I crowned a crab, that made me confess.
With each little wave, my worries did fade,
A castle of laughter, beach antics displayed.

As the sun dipped low, I let out a cheer,
Tomorrow's fun waits, never a fear.
With marigold dreams, I'll dance and prance,
On this goofy shore, I'll take a chance.

Elysian Breezes

Oh, the wind whispers secrets so bright,
While my hat takes a flight, a comical sight.
Chasing it down, what a wild crew,
A dog joined the chase, that cheeky shrew!

Finding a coconut, my drink of delight,
Tried to crack it open—what a fright!
Instead of sweet milk, it spewed like a hose,
I slipped in the chaos, right on my nose!

Beach volleyball game turned into a mess,
My friend served the ball, but it hit my dress.
Laughter erupted, I joined in the fun,
In this silly moment, my worries undone.

As evening descends, and the sky blazes red,
I'll dance with the waves, make dreams in my head.
Elysian breezes, so cheerful and bright,
With each laugh and giggle, everything's right.

Dappled Dawn Dreams

The dawn breaks softly, waves wink and play,
I've spilled my coffee, oh what a day!
A pelican swoops, right past my snack,
With crumbs on my face, I can't take it back.

Sandwiched between two sunbathing squirrels,
I tried to sunbathe, but they gave me swirls.
Acorns start bouncing, what's in the air?
A patch of giggles, a floating affair.

My flip-flops squeaked with each gleeful step,
I tried to shout, but instead, I just crept.
A crab did the cha-cha, in shades of pink,
I joined in the jive, much to my wink.

Dappled dawn dreams in hues so bright,
With each mischief shared, we'll party all night.
Laughter is music, in sandy retreat,
With silly sea antics, life feels so sweet.

Coastal Hues of Happiness

On the shore where the laughter won't cease,
Sandcastles crumble, yet we build with ease.
A jellyfish waved, but I jumped in fright,
Thought it was a beach ball—what a delight!

Shells and treasures scatter like stars,
We played hopscotch, avoiding the jars.
A seagull swooped down, seeking a bite,
Stole my sandwich, oh what a sight!

Under umbrellas, I chuckle and sigh,
As sunscreen drips like a pie in the sky.
A sunburned nose and a laugh so bright,
With coastal hues of happiness, wrong feels right.

At dusk, we danced under stars that gleam,
With our goofy adventures, we sail on a dream.
Life's funny surprises, like waves in the sea,
In these coastal moments, we're wild and free.

Sunbeams on Soft Sand

A crab in shades, strutting with flair,
It dances like it hasn't a care.
Seagulls gossip over a lost fry,
While sunblock fights off a burn quite spry.

Kids scream loudly just to complain,
Pulling their dads in the water's domain.
Flip-flops flying, nothing quite right,
While beachballs launch into full flight.

Beach blankets spread like a picnic feast,
Mom's sandwich swipes a seagull's least.
Sandcastles topple, a grand royal mess,
Pails and shovels—a grainy success.

The tide rolls in, what a funny show,
Chasing the feet of folks in a row.
Laughter erupts with each splashing wave,
As everyone waves goodbye to the cave.

Radiant Relations

Auntie's hat flies with the breeze,
Screaming, "Help!" from the tall palm trees.
Uncle's flip-flops squeak like a song,
While kids skateboard where they don't belong.

Cousins with sunscreen, a ghostly sight,
Trying to blend in, they're pure delight.
Chasing each other, a silly brigade,
Until someone face-plants in the shade.

Granny sips lemonade, a wise, sweet sip,
Moans about youths and their wild trip.
Her beach chair, a throne with comfy allure,
While granddad's broiling—oh! He's not demure.

Laughter erupts as a wave plops down,
Bathing suits soaked, they all wear a frown.
Yet smiles break through, as they share the ride,
In family craziness, they take great pride.

The Art of Ocean Light

Sunshine spills like a spilled can of paint,
As surfers bumble, a sight, not quaint.
Their boards flip wild, and oh the strife,
Like fish on land, they're struggling for life.

Seashells whisper secrets of the sea,
About the mermaids, they wish to be.
But seagulls come, with their honks and jibes,
Turning the shells into fabulous bribes.

Fried doughnuts glisten in golden beams,
While ice cream cones drip like pizza dreams.
Sandwiches vanish, a pitiful feat,
Are you done? Who will take just one seat?

Yet laughter lingers on salty air,
As joy erupts everywhere, everywhere.
The tide may roll, but so does fun,
In the merry chaos, we're still number one!

Saltwater Symphony

A saxophone croons, wrapped in the breeze,
As waves clap back, playing with ease.
Towels spread out, a colorful show,
While coolers pop like a summer piano.

Barefoot dances on the warm golden ground,
While children are lost, laughter's profound.
A beach ball soars, hitting a folk,
A trumpet blast makes everyone croak.

The frisbee flutters, floats with the wind,
A cat chasing it, trying to blend.
But with all this chaos, one can't deny,
In this wild life, they're simply flying high.

So here's to beach days, laughs loud and clear,
To the joy of the sun, and maybe a beer.
As saltwater rhythms play in our hearts,
We'll dance in the chaos, that's how the fun starts.

www.ingramcontent.com/pod-product-compliance
Lightning Source LLC
Chambersburg PA
CBHW050317100526
44585CB00016BA/1516